The Space Between the Notes

The Space Between the Notes
by
Dr. Richard A. Wing

HB Publications
Mobile, Alabama

THE SPACE BETWEEN THE NOTES

Copyright © 1994 by Richard A. Wing

ISBN 0-940882-20-5

First Edition

Cover design by Melissa M. Bowden
Book design by Tom Mason Communications

Manufactured by Walsworth Publishing Company,
Marceline, Missouri, United States of America.

HB Publications
P.O. Box 2806
Mobile, Alabama 36652
(334) 432-6606

Correspondence with Dr. Wing should be directed to:
First Community Church
1320 Cambridge Blvd. • Columbus, Ohio 43212
Phone (614) 488-0681

Dedicated to my father,
Robert H. Wing,
1911-1994

ACKNOWLEDGMENTS

I wish to acknowledge my Aunt Ermee Dixon of Atlanta, Georgia; Guy and Virginia Pearson of La Jolla, California; Harold Zieg and Karl and Babs Case of Columbus, Ohio, for their encouragement and commitment to the publication of this book.

I especially lift up the encouragement and love of my wife, Shirley Evans Wing, whose patience and insight are the greatest of all blessings on my spiritual path.

Introduction

An old man taught me how to play the mandolin, which I play, not very well, to this day. Right in the middle of a lesson he stopped suddenly. "What do you think is the most important thing to know about music?"

After a few missed guesses on my part, he relished saying with toothless grin, "It is not the notes you play that make the music. The music is made by the space between the notes." He was talking not only about music but about all life. The title of this book belongs to the humble San Francisco octogenarian man named Rudy Cipolla. In time, when I thought about the space between the notes, I thought more about life than music.

I have come to realize two things at mid-life. First, life is understood backwards but must be lived forwards. Second, there are no big deals anymore. Greatness is to be found in the common and everyday experiences of life or not at all. It is also true that we must go a long distance before realizing this truth.

The Hassidic masters told the story of Isak of Krakow. Isak, a humble Jew, wished for greatness. He

wanted to build a house of prayer in his town of
Krakow. He was told, in a dream, to go to Prague and to
go to the bridge that entered the king's castle. In the
dream, he was told to dig underneath the bridge where
he would find gold, and with that gold he could build
the house of prayer.

So, Isak went to Prague. He started digging under
the bridge that went to the king's castle, and was caught
by a guard. Stunned by his capture, he decided the truth
would serve him best. He told the story of his dream and
his journey in search of gold. "What a laugh," cried the
guard. "Let me tell you of my dream last night," said the
guard. "I had a dream last night that I went to the house
of a Jew in Krakow and moved the stove in his kitchen
and found a box of gold underneath it. Now, do you
think I am stupid enough to go to Krakow and try to
find one of many Jews named Isak and find the gold?"
Isak was released and returned to Krakow and went into
his home and moved the stove and underneath the floor
he found the gold with which he built a house of prayer.

The moral of the story is this: everything you need
or want is inside you or near you. However, you must
go on a very long journey to discover that truth.

The hope of finding the sacred wedged between the
moments of everyday life is the reason I write. I will
journey through the quarter notes of childhood and
adolescence, then to the whole notes of adulthood and
finally the grace notes, without which there is no hope.

Richard A. Wing

Chapter 1
QUARTER NOTES

The glasses through which we move into adulthood have lenses that were ground in childhood, where we learned the quarter notes of life.

In that first quarter of life, I did not think much was going on of any lasting significance. Now, in looking back and naming the imprints of childhood on my memory, I have discovered that more was there than what I thought. I have discovered the music that was wedged in between my boredom, rebellion, and my delight that was a part of growing up. Looking back, I have found the quarter notes to be more sacred and important than I had imagined at the time.

DEATH IS NOT A BIG DEAL, BUT
REFUSING TO BE YOURSELF IS

I was not more than eight years old when I tasted death for the first time. My great-grandmother died at ninety-four years of age. I remember the funeral in a farming community. Fans were going overhead, and hand-held fans supplied by the funeral home were flapping in the hands of most of the folk there.

Afterward my father said he would go with me by the casket like everyone else was doing and pick me up so I could see. What I saw, I didn't like. I knew then that I didn't like being around dead people. I especially knew I wouldn't like funerals of people that I knew.

When we got home, I announced for the whole family to hear: "I will never be a minister, because you gotta be around dead people." Counselors persuade people not to use two words: never and always. But life was simpler before counselors. I would *never* be a minister.

Much later in life I learned that it was not a big thing to be around dead people, but it is tragic being around alive people who are as good as dead. The greatest death of all is the refusal to be yourself.

Martin Luther King, Jr., said that the cessation of breathing does not mark your death. The moment you stop risking for love is the moment of your death. "The cessation of breathing is just a belated announcement of the death of the spirit that happened long ago" — the day you stopped being who you are.

Bessie Anderson Stanley said, "They have achieved success who have lived well, laughed often, and loved much; who have enjoyed — the love of children; who have filled their niche and accomplished their task; who have left the world better than they found it, whether an improved poppy, a perfect poem, or a rescued soul; who have always looked for the best in others and given them the best they had; whose life was an inspiration; whose memory a benediction."

Death in old age turned out not to be tragic. A person's refusal to be who they are remains the greatest grief of all.

WHEN GRANDMA WENT TO SEE
ORAL ROBERTS

In the mid-1950's the lights were slowly going out for my grandmother. She was slowly going blind with retinitis. The doctors said they could do nothing. You have no idea how much we wanted her to see. Grandma cried sometimes and felt like she wanted to die. I didn't know what to say when she told me she wanted to die.

One day I popped into my grandparents' apartment which was next to our house. I saw something I'd never seen before. The television was turned on to Oral Roberts who was now sweating profusely in the midst of doing supernatural things. He would grab people, smack his hand on them and scream "Jeeeezzussah — heal!" And, by golly, those people would walk away healed in Biblical proportions. In a big comfortable chair was my grandmother with her hand in the air as a sign of faith. I was frozen in the doorway at the sight of all this.

"Close the door, Richard," my grandfather said.

What followed was my watching miracles on television with one eye and my grandmother praying with arms in the air with my other eye. I was frozen with what I saw. Something new was happening in our family.

As my grandmother went slowly blind, she was also tuning in to Oral Roberts more on television. I started to watch with her.

The Space Between the Notes

Two things happened. First, I discovered, in myself, the most crystal clear faith that Grandma was going to get healed. Never could faith be so clear or so simple as the faith I had then. I would become incensed if anyone suggested that Grandma wouldn't and couldn't get healed. You don't know what a believer looks like until you look at my faith at ten years of age!

Time passed. Grandma got worse. The television healings continued. Then came hope.

I remember the day my grandfather announced that Oral Roberts was making a trip to California and was going to be nearby, and that Grandma was going to see him and get healed! They had to stay for the whole week of meetings. I was in school and could not go.

My grandparents left for the meeting. I prayed.

I noticed that my parents were concerned, because they wouldn't talk about the healing trip. I remember them looking for some way to help me with what they surely thought would be a letdown after Grandma's return. I remember them talking about a man in our church who did a study of people that went to Oral Roberts and discovered that he was a fake. I know that they feared that Oral, revealed as a fake, and Grandma's return, still blind, might really mess up my faith.

Meanwhile, I waited for the phone call and twenty/twenty vision!

Five days went by after my grandmother left home to visit Oral Roberts. No phone call came, but then again, my folks were frugal about long distance calls. At home we didn't talk about "the trip."

I always wondered what the people said in Biblical times after a healing. What do you say? I wondered what I would say when my grandmother came home healed. I normally asked for candy each time I saw her. I thought I should wait for a couple of days after she came home before asking for candy.

I came home from school at the end of the week. My grandparent's car was there. I went into our house and got the usual response and Graham Crackers from my mother. She said nothing about Grandma. I didn't ask. I went immediately to their apartment and walked in.

"What happened, Grandpa?"

Think of the word bitter and you will feel what followed. My grandfather angrily told me that to get there in the tent with Oral Roberts is not like seeing him on television.

"We were given a card and asked to describe what was wrong. The hopeless cases, like us, were all put together in one area. The ones that came up front to be on television were the ones with sickness in their heads. If they were convinced they were well, then they were well," my grandfather said with increased bitterness.

"And, the ones like your grandmother were asked to parade in front of Oral during the offering time," he continued.

"Did he say anything?" I asked.

My grandmother spoke for the first time. "All he did, Richard, was to say 'The Lord Bless you,' as we walked by. I turned toward where I thought he was and said, 'You're not the first one to say that to me.' 'Keep moving,' was all he said. And we did. Right out of the tent and into our car. We came home."

A long silence followed.

My grandmother lived another seven years after that and would die on the day that she got a good bill of

The Space Between the Notes

health from the doctor. She died of a broken heart and an inability to adjust to a very different world that went dark for her.

And I tell you this strange thing: Grandma's return altered my childhood faith not one bit! I couldn't figure out, right away, why I didn't believe any less when Grandma came home from Oral Roberts still blind.

Only time would teach me this: Faith turns out to be something quite apart from our hankering for magic at the hand of Jesus or Oral Roberts.

After the initial note of bitterness that she and my grandfather expressed, my grandmother resolved that she would die blind and that the sooner the better. Only once in a while was Oral Roberts ever referred to after that. Grandpa referred to him simply as "that fake."

As a child I thought faith was what one got when one saw miracles in Biblical proportions. When Grandma came home the same as before, and I realized my faith was unchanged, I began a long journey toward this truth: Faith is like a gift one receives, instead of a thing one works toward.

Miracles are, for some believers, an embarrassment and something they don't need for faith. Miracles for others are necessary and important.

Jesus did miracles for one reason — to produce faith. If you read the record, that program did not work too well. At best he was mistaken as to the response they would bring. At worst, he was blackmailed.

An old man told me, much later in life, why my faith did not change following Grandma's Oral Roberts journey. "Faith is a gift that has nothing to do with what happens to you," he said. "You can no more get faith

18

than you can get your Grandma well. A healing is a healing. Faith is a gift, often given when we are hurting a lot."

Grandma never got what she asked for, but she got an inner calm that led to her long desired death with peace.

Miracles aren't always getting what you want but getting what you need without knowing it. All this I could not see until long after Grandma went to see Oral Roberts.

NOISE IN THE NEIGHBORHOOD

I grew up in a neighborhood that I liked. I can tell you the name of everyone who lived in the ten houses that made up my neighborhood on Fiori Avenue and all of those who moved in and out while I lived there.

I slept in a bed by the window. One night I heard screams from a house two doors to the south. My brother did not awaken, and I went back to sleep.

The next day I went down the street to find two friends playing in the front yard. As if nothing new had happened, they took me to the door and showed me the 4-by-4 inch hole in it, created by a chair their father threw while drunk at 3:00 a.m. They were eating toast and seemed unconcerned. "It happens all the time," they said.

We played the usual games outside. Then the girls told me to come in and listen to "Flash Gordon" on the radio. I did. And there, in the kitchen nook, was their mother, with cigarette and coffee, and black and blue eyes that she tried to hide. When I walked into the kitchen, she was startled. "Dickie," she said, "don't tell no one. Please, don't tell no one what you see."

And I tell you this truth: I have not, until this day, told anyone anything about that day. And I had no idea that the sound in the night would be only the first of many like it that I would hear in my lifetime. The noise in the neighborhood was the reflection of a frustrated, unemployed, often intoxicated man, who dealt with his pain by taking it out on another human being.

It is good that we are talking more about family secrets that we were once asked to keep. Jesus said, "You shall know the truth and the truth shall make you free." And we are learning a more difficult truth: before the truth makes you free, it is going to make you mad as hell.

The noise in the neighborhood will not go away until we all face the pain of our own failed hopes, rather than inflict that pain on the ones we pledged to love.

SHAME WELL PLACED HAS A PLACE

I am convinced that things we want to forget are probably the things we must never forget.

I can remember the face of Mary Jane who sat across from me in the third grade. I can see her light green plaid dress covering her young overweight frame. I can see her red hair that didn't go with light green. I remember her large freckles — the kind with a lot of space between them. I can remember her talking slowly and not often, with a slight drawl that we connected to "someone from the south." I remember that she didn't do well in school. She was "slow." Most girls I knew in school made better grades than boys, but not Mary Jane.

The desire to belong got me involved in the group that would tease Mary Jane for no apparent reason. Kierkegaard said, "The crowd is untruth." The crowd does what no individual would do, and I would learn that a crowd could tease the way none of us would individually.

Mary Jane taught me the importance of shame for the right reason.

Mary Jane smelled funny. From neglect, no bath or whatever, she smelled. Rather than ignore that fact, we kids made a game of it. We decided that the smell was catching. Hence, you could play tag and pass the smell on from one to the next. And so we did. She did not know the reason for the laughter or what our cruel game played out on the school ground was all about. Robert Fulghum talks about everything we need to know being learned in kindergarten. I must add that there are many cruel things found on the same playground where Fulghum found virtue.

Suddenly, for one week, Mary Jane did not come to school. The cruel game and laughter went on without her. The following week our teacher called for silence in the classroom to make an announcement.

"You have perhaps noticed that Mary Jane has been gone for a week. She will be coming back next week. I need to tell you that she has been away because her mother died of cancer after a long illness. Mary Jane has been doing all of the work in the house including the cooking and washing. Please welcome her back when she comes next week."

The silence was deafening and indicting. The silence in the class must have been like the silence that Mary

Jane met each day after school, as she went home to an empty house and a mother dying in a hospital across town.

When Mary Jane came back to class, I approached her slowly. "I'm sorry about your Mom," I said as if reading words from a note pinned to my shirt.

"It's OK now," she said. "We will get by better now because she don't hurt no more."

And why I went to the far end of the playground and cried where no one could see, I could not figure out. Only later could I realize that I had encountered shame and had fallen into the hands of forgiveness all at the same time.

I would not see Mary Jane at school any longer because she moved. But I shall never forget her face, and the game, and the death, and the tears, and the shame and the forgiveness.

NAME CHANGE

A new kid moved in on our block when I was eight years of age. He was of Asian ancestry. It didn't take us kids more than one day to ask innocently, "Norman, are you a China man?"

"No! I am Filipino!," he would answer. We kids thought all Asians were Chinese. Norman looked Chinese to us so we called him that.

Eventually, Norman became one of my best friends. He lived with his grandparents, who were very old. I asked him where his mom and dad were. He would always change the subject when I asked. I finally stopped asking, and I knew he was relieved.

Norman's house was a good place to play because his grandparents weren't concerned about how much we messed things up. I assumed they were religious since there was a cross on the wall with Jesus hanging on it.

I think Norman Cabaluna and his grandparents liked me, because I was the first one to whom they told their family secret.

"Well what's up?" I said as I plunged into the couch at their home. Norman and his grandparents got rather ceremonial.

"We are now citizens of this the United States of America," they said.

"That's it?," I said. I thought everyone who wanted to belonged to the USA just by showing up. Norman's grandfather cried a little.

"And, Dick, we want you to know that we have a new last name. Our last name now is Anderson. We are no longer Cabalunas, but Andersons."

"But I like Cabaluna," I blurted out.

"We are now Americans and our last name is Anderson," they persisted.

I called Norman by his new name after that, but every time I said "Hey, Anderson!" I knew I liked Cabaluna better. And still do to this day. I know that Norman knew that what he wanted — i.e. to blend into the neighborhood — would not happen by changing his name. I yearned that day for a place where diversity is not a curse demanding change, but an opportunity that calls for delight and celebration. I yearn still.

The Space Between the Notes

THE DAY I MET THE PRINCESS

All of us have childhood heroes. Some heroes disappoint us when we know too much about them. The image of other heroes stays intact even after we know more about them.

The hard part about childhood heroes is when they don't turn out to be all they are cracked up to be. My wife had "Cactus Jim" who told kids to eat three bites of everything on their plate. My childhood friend from Idaho had "Sheriff Spud" who taught good things, most of which involved potatoes.

And I had the best hero of all: Princess Pat.

Princess Pat was pretty, and I think I fell in love with her like some boys do their third grade teacher. She wore a "real" princess dress, had a crown, a wand and shoes with sparkly things on them. She was no fake princess — she was a "real" princess.

Our local shopping center announced that she was coming to visit one Saturday. I was ecstatic. I counted the days and was among the first to get there to see Princess Pat. My brother teased me by telling me she was fake and an actress. I condemned his unbelief.

I arrived at the shopping center very early. It turned out that I got there too early.

I didn't join the crowd waiting for Princess Pat in front of the drugstore, but went behind another store to wait for her arrival. Behind the store was a little trailer that was brought in as a dressing room for the Princess.

Out of that trailer, out of view of everyone, except me, Princess Pat stepped, complete with her dress on, and a *cigarette*! Princess Pat *smokes*! The hero of my life! The instructor of children on how to eat, sleep and be good! Miss Right! I excused the Keds she was wearing before appearing, but *smoking*! Princess Pat, how could you?!

As the crowds flooded around her later, I approached, taking my turn for her autograph. On television, I thought she was twenty years of age. Up close, I saw the heaviest layer of make-up I had ever seen in my life! How could I have fallen in love with this old woman! I must be sick!

I moved forward, got the autograph, smelled the smoke all over her, went to my bike, and left with one less hero in my life. I went home and looked at my pictures of Roy Rogers and Dale Evans, who, someone told me, in real life, are Christians and don't smoke *or* cuss!

The best thing about a hero is to be found when you keep them at a distance. There is a real risk when you bring them up close and measure them against the values of your childhood home. You might just lose them under such severe examination.

I can laugh at my tough standard for my hero back then. But I could not laugh that day as I rode home, alone and lonelier than I had ever been.

SAM

I first met my Uncle Sam in 1957 when he drove into my hometown in a new Cadillac, took me to the store and bought toys. I didn't understand his work but knew he made more money than most people.

As we headed to the toy store I asked, "Uncle Sam, are you rich?"

He laughed loudly, then answered nervously.

"Richard, my boy, depending on how things go in the near future, I am going to be either the richest or poorest relative you will ever have." He laughed again.

As we pulled up to Trains 'n' Planes, the toy store, I told him that I hoped he would get rich. "We'll see," was his only reply as we went shopping.

I didn't see him again until 1976, on an island, after he had "made it" quite well. I wasn't on the island for more than an hour when he said, "I want to tell you about the man who changed my life." I pulled up a chair.

My uncle was one of these fast-track businessmen who was always in movement, pushing, pulling and making a new deal. A man who worked in his warehouse for over twenty years watched his movements.

One day this man had enough courage to stop Sam in his tracks. "Mr. Sam, I want to talk to you!" The man walked out to the edge of the property and stopped in front of a rock.

"Mr. Sam," he said, sounding much like a black preacher from the South whose authority you do not question. "Mr. Sam, do you see this rock? This rock was here millions of years before you came to this earth, and it is going to be here millions of years after you leave. You could be here an average age of say, seventy-four years, or shorter, or longer. We don't know. But, I tell you, Mr. Sam, you're gonna have to decide whether you will break your life over this rock by running around so much or if you will sit down on it once in a while and smell the roses and enjoy this place while you're here."

A long silence settled over them.

"That's all, Mr. Sam." The warehouseman left Sam and went back to work.

Once in a great while, we are struck by words we don't want to hear but need to hear. Those moments are both sacred and difficult, and they don't come often.

"That man changed my life, Richard," said my uncle as we sat on his boat in the Bahamas, looking at his home in the Cay, twenty years after going to the toy store.

Oh, sure, he made money. But he didn't make a life until he was touched by that man in his warehouse.

"What does it profit a person, if they gain the whole world and lose."

The next lesson took place on my uncle's boat.

"Happiness," he said.

"What?" I said, over the roar of engines.

"Happiness! What is it?" he demanded.

I felt like I was back in the third grade.

"See that island?" He pointed. "Everyone who lives on it is a millionaire. And you know what? Just being a millionaire didn't get 'em happy. I have looked at this thing for a long time. I have noticed that the ones who inherited their money are a bunch of drunks. The ones who had to struggle not only appreciate what they have but are able to handle it better and take joy in giving it away."

I listened.

"Unhappy and miserable is how I find many of them," he said. "And what makes for happiness?"

I waited. He went on.

"You find it inside yourself — it is something you do yourself — for yourself — no one else can do it for you. You find happiness inside yourself or not at all."

The lesson was finished.

Some people try to live at Mardi Gras all their life with the intention of never undertaking the very deep look at oneself that is demanded the day after every party is over.

"The unexamined life is not worth living."

Sam taught me that in his simple reflections on his own life.

TEACHERS

My colleague and friend Bill McNabb has a great knowledge of English literature — Shakespeare, Dante and Milton. His knowledge and love of these greats amazes me.

"When did you learn so much about English literature?" I asked one day.

"From Mrs. Mortensen," he replied.

Mrs. Mortensen was four feet eleven in heels. As a teacher of high school seniors, she had one shot, she believed, one year at most, to place in the hearts of students a love of Shakespeare, Dante and Milton. Her love for writers was contagious, and Bill remembers her reciting, by memory, some of their greatest passages, with eyes closed, holding even restless seniors spellbound.

Bill was one year into college and noticed that he knew things others did not know — namely, Shakespeare, Dante and Milton. He wrote a letter to Mrs. Mortensen and thanked her. She did not write back.

Two years later, while on vacation, Bill ran into Mrs. Mortensen in the grocery store. "Do you remember me, Mrs. Mortensen?"

"Billy McNabb, of course I remember you!"

"Did you get my letter?" Bill asked.

"Yes I did," she replied and took it out of her purse, right there in front of the vegetables.

Bill mistakenly said, "After teaching forty years, I'll bet you have gotten a lot of letters from former students."

"Two, to be exact," was her response, and she produced the other letter from a slot in her purse that was now empty.

The gift of gratitude is all that is needed for those who, through sacrifice, pain, effort and prayer, made a difference in our lives. We think those who loved us and taught us well know that they taught us well, but they don't. Gratitude answers the nagging question, "Did I do any good all those years I taught?"

In the ninth grade, weird was the name that I gave anyone who was different from me or didn't like me. That was what I called Mrs. Angelinoff, who knew history and desired that I know it too.

She spoke with an accent, and we loved to imitate her during lunch time. She was from Bulgaria. God only knows where that is, and we didn't care. She had wire rim glasses that slid down her nose when she taught us world history with a passion and urgency that baffled us. We were unmoved. We were concerned about life going on without Buddy Holly, Richie Valens and the Big Bopper — all killed one night in Clear Lake, Iowa.

Mrs. Angelinoff talked about freedom from the perspective of one who lost it during World War II. She told us why we should not throw a bite of food away.

We were unmoved by all her oddities and didn't pay attention. Until one day.

This diminutive teacher was talking about World War II and began to tell of the bombings of her apartment building. She told of her fear. She told of the sirens. She told of screaming and running to the basement for many days.

"One day I ran down the stairs screaming into the basement," she said, "when all of a sudden, I stopped. People ran by me, but it did not matter. I looked out the window and saw the bombs being dropped even on the cemetery — bombs bursting in air — bombs dropping everywhere." Her class was frozen with attention. Tears ran down her cheeks. "Then I remembered a scripture from the Psalms in my head: 'Be still and know that I am God.' And you know," she said, "from that day on, I was never afraid, and I did not scream again."

Silence remained for at least a minute.

I was the paper boy for Mrs. Angelinoff. Even when I was collecting for the newspaper, she would remind me "never to waste food." I lied and said I wouldn't. And every month while I made those rounds she would lecture me on being appreciative of my country.

Today, at ball games, mostly when we sing "the rockets red glare," I see her face sometimes and hear her broken English. And I thank God for letting her believe that she was getting through to me, even though she wasn't at the time.

Most of all I give thanks for her telling of the **faith that found her while screaming down the stairway of death, because we will be, all of us, somewhere on that stairway someday.**

Mrs. Angelinoff is dead now. And the knowledge she stored grows in the attic of my memory. I am thankful for her face and her accent and her lecture and her life.

Quarter Notes

As a junior in high school, I sat across the aisle from George Lucas, the creator of *Star Wars*. The class was Public Speaking 101 with Mrs. Speltz as the teacher.

Poor George died every time he got up to speak because he was quiet, introverted, and spent most of his time reading science fiction comics rather than studying. A kid like that isn't going to amount to anything for sure!

But to this day, my hero is Mrs. Speltz who taught both George and me. On a routine day in class I was asked to do a humorous reading. She asked to see me after class.

"Close the door," she said. Her face was red, and I thought she was angry. Without my saying a word she demanded, "Where have you been?"

I didn't know what she meant. I had not been given the recommendation by my eighth grade English teacher to take speech class because she said, "That is something you will never do well, so just forget it." Mrs. Speltz wondered why I had waited until my third year of high school to take a basic speech course.

Mrs. Speltz said, "I don't care where you've been. I know where you're going! I need you to compete in Humorous Interpretation on our speech team. You are going to compete this Saturday. Be here at 9:00 a.m.!"

She had faith in a kid who was lost. District meetings were followed by the State Championship, which I won, because of her faith in me when I needed it most. I handed my trophy to her in gratitude. The greatest gift of a teacher is in the moment they believe in you when others apparently don't and, most especially, when you don't believe in yourself.

The Space Between the Notes

When I walked onto the stage to give my humorous interpretation speech in the state finals in 1961, I did not know that Tina was dead. Not until back at the motel room, while jumping up and down with my friends, was the call to come. My parents spoke in halting tones. They were not in celebration.

"Tina is dead." Tina Hanson, young and beautiful, classmate since fifth grade, friend in church youth group — Tina was dead. She walked to the school office at the same time I walked onto the stage to give my final speech. She was treated for a headache by the school nurse. When she fell to the floor, an ambulance was called, and she didn't last the night.

The best day of my life became one of the worst.

In two days I was marching to school carrying a trophy. In four days I was marching to a grave carrying her casket.

Weeks later, I was reading Thornton Wilder's classic, *Our Town*. Before Tina's death, I could not get the point of the play. After her death, I could finally hear it.

The stage manager speaks: "Now there are some things we all know, but we don't take 'em out and look at 'em very often. We all know that something is eternal. And it ain't houses, and it ain't names, and it ain't earth, and it ain't even the stars … everybody knows in their bones that something is eternal, and that something has to do with human beings. All the greatest people ever lived have been telling us that for five thousand years and yet you'd be surprised how people are always losing hold of it. There's something way down deep that's eternal about every human being."

The collision of the best and worst moments of life is the same place that we get glimpses of the eternal.

Courage is needed in that moment and leaves no room for the timid.

There was a teacher, a professor, who I felt hated me and ended out helping me. I say "I felt" because most often reality doesn't count with professors or teachers, but what we feel does. I don't really know if this professor hated me, but it felt that way, and that is all you need at a young age in order to indict the very person who wants to help you.

The class was college freshman English. The work was mainly composition. In high school, I had a teacher who liked me and made me think I was a good writer. My mistake was believing her. By the time I got to college and discovered that the professor was going to teach us to write, or else, I knew I was playing in a different league. I was scared and in deep trouble.

Our first composition was due. I went after the subject with the same expertise that I used as a junior in high school. The paper came back with red all over it.

"It would be best for you to simply start all over again," the professor said. He explained all the rules I had violated.

"Intransitive what, sir?," I said. I didn't understand anything he explained.

"Start over again. It's OK to start over." The words rang in my ears until I reworked it five times in order to get a low "B."

When you are young, you hate anyone who makes you start over.

Twenty-five years later, very casually, I mentioned to a fellow student the name of the one who I thought hated me and, in fact, helped me the most.

"He's dead you know. He killed himself," my friend said.

"Start over. Start over. It's OK to start over."

The gift he gave me in life is the gift I hope he found after his final exit.

Chapter 2
WHOLE NOTES

Getting away from where you spend the first quarter of your life is the first step toward looking at life with wider lenses.

In the quarter time of life, we get the mistaken idea that the whole creation is like us, or if not, it ought to be. I know a man who grew up in the mid-west who said that going away to college was the realization that the way he was and the way he did things in his small town "were not God."

On the other hand, the whole of life is found by looking closely at life's individual parts wherever you go. If we can tune ourselves to listen to whole notes wherever we are, without making our own quarter notes the measuring stick of creation, the greater gifts of life can be received.

The first step toward the whole picture came for me when I met a variety of people who lived in a small rural valley in Oregon. I served as minister of a little congregation while attending a small college that trained ministers. The moments with these people, I thought, were moments wherein I was only biding time, waiting for greater life experiences to come my way. Looking back now, I realize that whole notes were being played at exactly the moment I thought nothing was happening.

I
THE RIDGE

I was a student minister at a little church along the ridge of the Mohawk Valley in Springfield, Oregon, between 1963 and 1966. The lessons I learned there were an important part of the whole story I couldn't get any other place.

At the end of my life, I doubt that I will have learned more than at this beginning moment with the people who lived on the ridge of the valley. T. S. Eliot warned that this is so:

> What we call the beginning is often the end
> And to make an end is to make a beginning.
> The end is where we start from …
> We shall not cease from exploration
> And the end of all our exploring
> Will be to arrive where we started
> And know the place for the first time.
> T. S. Eliot, *Four Quartets*

The first funeral I ever did was in 1963 for a former Southern Baptist named George who was bitter because of bad theology and something else he wouldn't tell me about at first. For openers, he said he hated me and would tell me why in time.

I had no idea where the conversation and pilgrimage in this poor valley was going to lead me. I was confused and committed enough to keep showing up even though I knew I didn't know what to say. He wasn't conforming to anything I read in books. He began talking about his inevitable death.

I drove up to George's house for my second visit and my first lesson.

Without knowing it, George was about to teach me this truth: **the issue is *never* the issue**. *Most often* what people say the problem is, is not the problem at all. Most of the time what people verbalize as the problem is only the surface language used to point to pain so deep that to look at the real issue would be to die.

I approached George's bedroom for the second time, still wondering why he didn't like me. At that young age, being liked was the only thing that counted.

The room had the smell of wetness from seeping rain. George asked me to sit down.

"I hate organized religion," he said. He wasted no time picking up from last time. My first thought was, I wonder if he likes disorganized religion better. I didn't respond.

"And, I especially don't like ministers. I think the whole bunch, ministers and church folk, are hypocrites!"

At the same time I was working as minister of a country church, I was also selling shoes on Fridays and Saturdays. At that moment the shoe business looked better than ministry.

As a minister, George doesn't like me and wants nothing to do with the church. But, if I were to meet him in the shoe store, it is pretty clear that he came because he needed shoes. The shoe business looked better all the time because of its clear agenda when you enter the store. Clean and clear — you need shoes — I sell 'em. In the church, most of the time you don't know what people need, and then when you offer what you have, it isn't what people want ... or need.

George's wife, who was a member of my church, ushered me to the door in the hopes that I would come back even though George was pretty tough on me. I lied and said I would love to come back.

"Incidentally, Dick," she said as I went for the door, "it is not you he hates. The minister of his church ran off with his wife twenty years ago. It is not you he is hating. He just doesn't know how to get rid of the pain from the past. Most things we say we're angry about are really caused by something else, but of course you know that." She closed the door. I left puzzled.

That lady with a third grade education gave me the first most important thing that I needed to know in ministry — the issue is never the issue.

The second thing I learned from George was the fact that we tend to criticize others to the same degree that we have personal pain. After some time in ministry, it has become clear to me that Jesus' urging for us not to judge others is not only because it doesn't help others, but because we have this penchant for **criticizing in others that which is our own weakness**.

Some of the most self-righteous speeches I have ever heard about how bad others are, were from persons I visited in prison. We just seem to judge others for the same weaknesses in us, and hence, the word from Jesus is to not judge because we don't know how to do it.

George softened, in time, and was able to tell me in his own words why he did not like me or any minister.

"Because a minister ran away with my wife once, long ago."

"I can see why you would hate so much," I said. We were silent for what seemed a long time.

"But that is all over now, Dick," George said, "so why don't you and I be friends right now, because you know I'm dying and I don't want to go out with a grudge." George liked teaching me.

When I visited next, George was in a different mood. He had moved from concern about himself and shifted the concern to his neighbor. "Would you go see my neighbor? She has gone crazy from listening to a radio preacher!" I told him I would call on her soon. Soon turned out to be sooner than I expected.

As I left George's home, the neighbor lady opened the front door of her house and a billow of smoke came out and I thought the place was on fire.

"Need the fire department?," I yelled.

"No! This place isn't on fire. And unless we get back to living and believing, like in the olden days, we are all going to burn!"

I made the mistake of approaching her. I was about to meet a woman with a forty-pound Bible and a smoke-filled house.

"My name is Dick, and I am George's minister and I was wondering if … "

"This world is going to hell," she interrupted. "Unless we get back to living like olden days, we're going to burn! I just got my wood stove today and got it going. I didn't know you needed a smoke stack first before lighting it."

Later George told me that this woman moved from San Francisco to Oregon in order to be in the town where the ministry of a famous radio preacher started. She turned her head, hands and money over to this preacher. I'm not saying he said it, but she heard him say that we needed to live like they did in the last century to be good before God. She also believed that we needed to work hard to make it to heaven, but it was doubtful that after our best efforts we would make it.

She was not mentally well. I could not make logical conversation. Mental illness combined with religious fervor is lethal. She was taken away a few days later, and I returned to visiting George each day until his death.

George died. The funeral plans were made. We were to have the service at a local mortuary. I had to borrow money to get a black suit and tie to go with my black Bible. That essential equipment would do me no good.

George chose me as the only visitor he wanted to have during the months of his drawn-out death. Continually by his side were his wife and stepdaughter. I remember only one reference to George having relatives. His relatives had nothing to do with him after he started drinking a little bourbon each day and got divorced.

And, lo and behold, when his death hit his home state of Arkansas, his relatives — all of them, came rushing to Oregon for the big funeral. I was baffled by this. He had been condemned and rejected by relatives who would not send one card or make one phone call or any contact with him but who would come running across the country at his death.

The service lasted thirty minutes. I went to the back of the chapel as the family came forward. That Arkansas group made a ring around the casket, fell on it, started weeping and moaning and all praying at the same time.

"Do you know these people?" demanded the funeral director.

"No," I said as I turned pale.

Up front, there was more weeping, wailing and falling on the casket, which by now was beginning to tip and pivot. The funeral director blurted out the name of our Lord and Savior and ran to the front. He caught the casket just before it hit the floor. He called for me and an assistant, and we tipped it back up on the stand. The wild praying didn't stop during all this. I was stunned. The director was sweating profusely. I thought about how easy it is to sell shoes compared to this.

Soon, in the hearse the director looked over at me and said, "How many funerals have you done before?"

I replied, "This is my first."

"Well, I've done these for thirty years and this is the toughest one I've ever done. We almost lost George on the floor you know? Who are those people?"

I learned that day that guilt leads us across the nation to weep and wail for a dead relative. The weeping is not for the dead, but for ourselves for what we did not give while they were alive. And I did not know that day how many times I would see this same scene repeated.

In an old record book of mine the first name under "Funerals — 1963" is George Millican, to whom I would owe more than I knew on the day of his burial.

The funeral director soon quit and got into another line of work — used cars, I think. I kept going to school, not knowing that I would not learn much more than what I did from George and his life and his funeral.

The Space Between the Notes

II

I was asked to speak to the local Grange Number 133, in the valley along the ridge. Of all the ridiculous things, they would invite a local preacher on Sunday afternoon to come to a potluck dinner. That was fine. But after the dinner, they would ask the minister to get up and preach a "special sermon" to the local Grange at 2:00 p.m. on Sunday afternoon. As I watched polite heads nod off to sleep, I told more jokes without gaining any "awakenings." One guy in the back got whiplash after his wife nudged him, and he popped up like an English muffin in a wide-mouthed toaster. She poked him right when he began to snore. She whispered reprimands that everyone could hear. I swear they were all asleep when I finished after talking fifteen minutes — a preview of things to come.

Mr. Quigley was there that day and was on my list of neighborhood calls to make. I heard two things about him — he was interesting, and he was rich. Oh yes, a third — he was not the faintest bit interested in church. I told him I would come by to see him, and he said he would be glad to have me.

I drove into his huge driveway and went to the door. I was well received and ushered into the longest ranch-style house I have ever seen in my life, framed outside with rambling white fences and horses everywhere.

"You shouldn't be here," he said, "but I'm glad you are." I didn't know what he meant.

After iced tea, a tour of the big house, talk of horses, and a donation of food for a needy family, he began to talk about what I wanted to hear. You see, Mr. Quigley was at Pearl Harbor on December 7, 1941. He was also the first one to radio out the word of the attack. I was in rapt attention for an hour and was well rewarded with stories I shall never forget. Finally, I got up to leave.

"You shouldn't be here," he repeated.

"Where should I be?," I naively asked him. He didn't answer. Instead he drew a map of a dirt road going up the mountain. He gave me a large basket of food.

"Take this up the hill to this family. That's where you ought to be. If the church would do what Jesus said to do with the poor, you couldn't hold the number of us that would beat a path to your door."

With those mysterious words, a rich man handed me food and a map and persuaded me up the hill.

III

After driving up a terrible dirt road, I finally came to an old house. The only clear memory I have to share is that it was winter and the window frames were empty and the doorway was a breezeway.

I started walking, with the food, to where the door was supposed to be. A man with seven children timidly came out. They greeted me in a huddle. I introduced myself and told them I was bringing food on behalf of our church in the valley. They thanked me while mostly looking at the ground.

"How do you get along here in this house with no windows and doors?" I asked.

"With lots of love," he said as one of his little girls got closer to him. "My wife died of cancer and I got the kids now, and we get along on not much stuff, but on a lot of love."

Soon I left.

I drove by Mr. Quigley's house on the way back to let him know I made the delivery. I secretly wondered still why he didn't go himself.

"Why don't you go up there yourself, Mr. Quigley?"

"Because he's a brother," he said.

"He's *your* brother!?" I gasped.

"No, he is *a* brother."

"I don't get it," I said.

"He was at Pearl Harbor with me on December 7, 1941. You can never be closer to anyone in life than those you fought with. And I wouldn't embarrass him by bringing him food, but I have to make sure he gets some because he is a brother."

He continued with a sermon without knowing it.

"You church folk get together, but nothing ever happens. You know why?"

I knew he was going to tell me anyway so I said, "Why?"

"I'll tell you. When you get together, you look like a family reunion where no one has been in contact with each other for twenty years and don't much care anyway. People at reunions have been ignoring or fighting with each other for years and ain't got much to say when they get together. But when you fight together *against* an enemy, no matter what your color, creed or politics, you are connected in a good way for life.

What you need in the church is something to fight for, instead of fighting with each other. Fight poverty — not each other! Then you will be close like you say you want to be, but ain't. Life has never been as good as when I was fighting with someone for something we believed in. Frankly, the rest of life has been a little boring compared to what we felt while fighting together in a foxhole."

Mr. Quigley preached well that day, and I left grateful.

IV

One of the things I learned the hard way at the first church I served in Oregon was this: never baptize a person downstream.

I have an Episcopalian friend who will remain unnamed. To this day, he likes to tease me about baptizing by immersion. He thinks it's kind of "untidy." But I tell you, you should see his office if you want to know what untidy is about. And to this day, he doubts this story I tell you that is exactly the way it happened.

I was lucky enough to serve a country church that did not have a baptistery inside and instead baptized right out in the Mohawk river in Biblical fashion.

I remember my first candidate for baptism. To the river, just a hundred yards from the church we went — all thirty-seven members of the church (we added one since last count). The candidate was female, rather heavy and dressed in a white baptismal robe. We waded out into the water and waited for the singing to stop.

I didn't know whether to baptize her with her head toward upstream or downstream. I decided, incorrectly, to baptize her with her head going the direction of downstream. When the current of a rushing spring river flows up a baptismal robe, you would not believe how fast that thing will float right over the candidates head and my hands.

The Space Between the Notes

So there we are in the river — me dipping and her robe flowing right over her head (yes, she had a swimming suit on). But, to come out of the water with a dripping gown caught over your head makes my Episcopal friend grin in a way that says, "untidy."

The only worse event was my youth minister, who, when asked to baptize his girlfriend, got flustered. He wasn't sure how to do this either. When he got to the middle of the river, he just grabbed her and put her under the water (start counting) and then made the pronouncement while she was under (keep counting): "Cindy, because of your confession of faith in Christ, and in obedience to his command, you are now baptized in the name of the Father, the Son … " by this time poor Cindy thinks she is forgotten on the bottom of the Mohawk River by a boyfriend intent on killing her.

When it came to "Holy Spirit" she raised herself out of that stream with a gasp like the sound of a mother when she hears that her daughter is pregnant at fifteen. Cindy stomped out of the river. The mood was definitely broken. Cindy and the youth minister didn't date much after that. He transferred to a trade school in Corvallis the next fall.

The Mohawk River is beautiful in the spring and is a cruel river for beginning clergy who don't know to baptize upstream and don't know to make the pronouncement before you dunk.

V

The man who fixed my car lived in the valley. He had a tune-up shop, believed in Jesus and attended AA meetings and liked to tell what the Lord had done for him. He never charged too much for a tune-up, was nice, uneducated, honest and said what he thought.

"I love Jesus but hate some parts of the church," said Ellis.

I knew I wouldn't be leaving soon when I said, "Oh yeah, how is that?"

"Judgmentalness," he said.

He continued. "I was a drunk once, Dick. No one knows the pain of being like that unless they been there. I hate, to this day, the times that people told me I needed to quit and judged me because I wouldn't, not knowing that I couldn't. You gonna be a preacher?"

I nodded.

"Well let me tell you something about judgin' people," he said with a sudden authority that surprised me. "Never judge. Never. That is God's business, not yours. Don't even let a person come close to thinkin' or feelin' that you are in charge of judgin' for God. We all have weaknesses, including you, and we all feel judged without you judgin' us."

"You need to get rid of this car, ya know?"

I nodded.

"Your job," he said, getting back to the lay-sermon, "is to find light in everyone. You ain't set up to judge, but to find light. Your job is to see that part, to find that part, even in the rottenest people. You don't know about the light that is buried deep in a rotten guy. That light is buried under pain, guilt and being treated bad. Your job is to peel off all that junk until you find the light in 'em. And everybody's got some. Some have only a little light buried deep — maybe just a spark. Don't matter. Your job is to find the spark even if that is all there is."

"Richard, my boy, you gotta get rid of this car. I'll fix it cheap, and you get rid of it."

And I did. And I didn't need his help any longer, but I kept dropping by to see him. Only in time would I realize that this suffering, honest, uneducated man would give me the best advice any preacher could get about pain, about judgment, and most important — about "the light" that shines in every child, every adult — everyone. "The light. Don't forget the light!"

VI

The only story I will not tell you about has to do with a couple that parked behind our church one Saturday night, got drunk and passed out. The next morning, right when everyone was gathering for worship, the truck was discovered. One man from our church went up to the truck, opened the door, and two sleeping naked bodies fell out on the ground and began to awake with much swearing. What was most interesting to me was how the Sunday school teachers explained the whole scene to the children next Sunday morning. One dear lady invited them to stay for the potluck dinner. They declined and drove away.

I shall never forget the valley with its mountains, its river and its people.

Chapter 3
GRACE NOTES

A grace note is when we know that things are all right at the center of existence even though, daily, we feel that everything is falling apart. Such a grace moment cannot be taught, made to happen or learned. Enough experience is needed to know that grace comes at the moment we are needy and vulnerable enough, and all our fix-it plans have been discarded at last.

Grace moments happened during the first quarter of my life. I could not recognize these gifts at the moment. Recognition came only in looking back. During the full notes of mid-life, grace moments were there. However, grace was not experienced because my hands were too full. My hands were full getting more of what I had enough of. My hands were full of achievement and nurturing others without reflection on my own inner desert.

Mine is not an unusual story but has much company. When we appropriately give up trying to make everything happen by our own effort, we begin to retrieve the grace notes of early life and mid-life, and live the last half of life as one prolonged act of grace.

Biblical specifics include Jesus in the boat with the disciples in the eye of the storm. The word from the disciples to Jesus is roughly "don't just sleep through this — do something!" When the words "peace, be still" are spoken, they are addressed to persons, not the weather. Grace note! We become acquainted with God who does not take us away from any of life's experiences but reminds us that God has blazed that trail before, and promises to go with us on ours. This is the most we get. And it is enough, even though we may not know it at the time.

Literary specifics include Kazanzakis' Zorba dancing on the sands of the beach after his great life project collapses around him. Dancing in the middle of disaster. Grace note! God meeting us in the center with the promised presence, while everything else falls apart.

Clinical specifics include the moment one walks into a therapist's office and announces, "My life has totally fallen apart!" The reply from the mid-wife of the soul is, "What a wonderful opportunity for growth that couldn't come any other way. Let's get started." Grace note!

What follows here are moments of utter loss, both tragic and comical, where grace notes show up in the midst of disaster, loss, pain and emptiness. These grace moments have names and faces. In these faces, I was found by the sacred.

Grace Notes

GLADYS

Most often we don't get what we want in life. Usually it is something else. The terrible part of this is that what we get is often much less than what we ask for. The up side is that what we get is often much better than what we knew to ask for. Garrison Keillor said, "That which we get is sometimes what we would have asked for in the first place, had we known."

Peggy Baker had a pen name of Gladys LeGrand. She was old and lived in a convalescent home. She summoned me to come to her bedside, presenting to me credentials that she was the daughter of a Disciple minister in Ohio. Even though she left the church in her late teens, never to return, she was indeed a believer and was a deeply spiritual person. So, I went not knowing under which name she was registered.

"Don't feel sorry for me," was her first command after I found her and we exchanged pleasantries.

"I have had a full life. I am in my nineties and can't move around, but I have a mind that works and that is full of memories. I love each memory and have learned to prize the bad ones now that I look back on them. Some of them are wild tales I love to tell." (And she told some, and they were wild!) "Just don't feel sorry for me!"

I put on my seat belt; I knew I was in for a ride.

Two claims to fame she had: she was a writer for Walter Winchell in the 1940's, and she had had a great amount of poetry printed in journals.

"What's this?" I asked as I looked at four stanzas of a poem on a poster on her wall.

"That's the only famous one I wrote," she replied. "It made *New Yorker Magazine*, *Time*, *Life* and a bunch of others."

The Space Between the Notes

The poem starts out by talking about one's choice in life to have a nice, quiet riding horse to go trotting along with through life. Just as the poem names exactly the kind of quiet horse that is wanted, the poem explodes:

> But as I spoke, a stallion, sable and proud,
> Broke from the woodland near with his long mane blowing.
> He was huge and swift as a storm-driven cloud,
> Fierce were his eyes as he galloped, his white teeth showing.
>
> Toward me he ran with fire from his nostrils streaming
> Stopped by my trembling side with a snort of thunder.
> Round his crimson bridle was graven in letters gleaming
> LIFE is my name. Ride me or be trampled under.
>
> *Gladys LeGrand*

"Good talking with you," she said. "Thanks for coming. You are my minister now. You may go now." All this in machine-gun style.

She was, for me, a prophet. Her prophecy stands true: To mount that wild ride is to be blessed. The courage to ride comes from strange places — even convalescent homes. Grace note!

IRMA

Early worship was beginning gradually. "We have come for a little quiet with you, O God." We began the informal liturgy.

From the back of the sanctuary, Rick informs us that his wife, Kay, working as a Hospice nurse, has just witnessed the death of a little four-year-old girl. The

52

family is poor and has no burial clothes, and Kay has asked that we help. Volunteers are many when we ask for help, both for clothes and money.

"We have come for a little quiet with you, O God."

In the same service, at the very same moment, Misty's beeper sounds. Misty is a chaplain at Hospice. She prepares to leave, but she discovers that the mother of the child who has just died speaks Spanish and little English. Vicki with fluent Spanish leaves with Misty to interpret. Worship continues.

"We have come for a little quiet with you, O God."

We all move to the Annual Meeting of the church. Good food! Good reports! Good goals! Good officers! Good grief — time to quit! Late service to begin.

Misty comes to the back of the church after the annual meeting. A message is brought to me at the pulpit. There is a need for seventy-five dollars for the mortuary to take care of Irma Espinoza. I guarantee to my messenger that the money has already been collected.

"We have come for a little quiet with you, O God."

Note on my desk on Monday reads: Irma will be viewed on Wednesday and have a graveside service on Friday.

Irma Espinoza, four years old, dead child — I write your name so that it will be read somewhere — so that hundreds of people will repeat your name and remember you as the infant intruder upon our worship, who led us to the face of God more quickly than all our hesitant preludes.

"We have come for a little quiet with you, O God!"

I remember when Barclay Wayne Deforest died. We were both ten years of age. On the very day that he drowned in a river, he gave me a knife that he knew I wanted. Before school, yelling at me to come over to his front yard fence, he gave me his knife as a sign of our friendship. And for years that knife sat in my cuff link box along with the cuff links I no longer wore. And every time I would see it, I would remember a life that deserved to be remembered.

For a while at least, we remembered Irma, whose death demanded our attention. She led us closer to God on the very weekend that we promised not to forget Martin Luther King's unfinished dream.

Grace note! Our liturgy was pointed to the needs of the poor, which is the only true liturgy that God desires repeated in his name.

"We have come for a little quiet with you, O God, and have left uncomfortable, and blessed. Amen."

CARLA

Hope is what Carla wanted on the phone. She called and said that she knows there is no hope for her relationship with her boyfriend. Since they had concluded that, they seemed to be getting along better as friends. But that is not really what she wanted. She wanted a friend who was also her husband. She was afraid to hope for more and afraid not to.

Vaclav Havel, the Czech playwright and president, said that he is not an optimist because he does not know that things will work out well. He, likewise, is not a pessimist because he does not know that things will work out poorly.

He concludes that hope is finally a gift. "Hope is an orientation of the spirit, an orientation of the heart. It is not the conviction that something will turn out well but the certainty that something makes sense, regardless of how it turns out."

I know people who have nothing to hope for and have within them a quiet spirit of contentedness and contentment that sometimes unnerves me. I can't figure out where their hope comes from. On the other hand, I know people who should easily be full of hope and joy, based on their talent, intellect and income, and they are not hopeful or joyful. A mystery.

I knew a woman in her late twenties who lived in the Midwest. She has hope and joy in her life now, but it has not always been that way. Her story she took time to tell me at a workshop I conducted.

"I had no hope," she began. The story went to drugs, many men, heavy drinking and many high-powered positions. Then, she was down and out because of excesses in all of the above. "I had no hope."

"Do you remember the story about the man who was as good as dead until his friends brought him on a stretcher to Jesus and lowered him through the roof?" she inquired. I nodded.

"Well, that was me. My friends saw how bad I was and literally took their hope and tackled me with it. I got mugged by hope! They went with me to a clinic and made me stay until I got well. If I had not had friends carry me to the healing source, I would be dead, now."

I was silent.

"Dick, there is nothing more like God in this world, than when your friends carry you to the healing source you cannot walk to yourself because of blurry eyes. It is beautiful when friends carry you on their hope when you don't have any."

Grace note! Mugged by hope! I shall never forget her face, or her story on the porch of a retreat house, or her friends lowering her through a roof in order to be healed.

LENT

Lee is dead.

I don't expect that to mean anything to you, yet.

On a December day, sometime in the night, Leland Regier died. I was ready to leave for a Christmas celebration with our volunteer staff when a friend called and said, "I don't know how to say this, but … "

I joined my wife for lunch. I told her. She said, "Oh no!" over and over. We then went silent. Neither of us knew how to cry yet.

Leland Regier was my best friend in ministry in Northern California. He was a preacher, teacher, pastor, cowboy, table tennis champ (do NOT call it ping pong, he said) and friend. He was fifty-seven years of age. He died of heart failure. His health had gone from terrific to poor in the short span of five years.

He *demanded* to see me the previous June. "I must see you," he *demanded*.

Listening with my pastoral ear, I promised, "I will be there in August and will spend an entire day with you. Is that soon enough?"

"Great," he said. And I did spend that day. The evening we ate dinner along the Delta with our wives. It was our last supper — our benediction banquet — our farewell for awhile, without my knowing it and with him knowing it all too well.

Grace Notes

Lee slams my life into Lent. I am sitting at my desk where his picture faces me and next to it is his date book, that I told him to buy eight years ago, complete with his handwriting and plans that go beyond the day that was his last. His wife Barbara gave it to me. And I don't expect my grief to be complete until I write this friend's life out of my system and into the hands of God. His death makes me tune into the difficult questions whose frequency is Lent.

A friend is someone you can say anything to and know that you will not be met with judgment but with grace notes.

Lee was a friend for me. Lunch is how we expressed friendship. Lee and I had a standing lunch commitment every Tuesday for nine years. That lunch was interrupted by vacations and funerals only.

Over lunch we would share the latest joke, sermon stories, names of those we held with deep concern, and most important, we told the truth about how life really was with us. I shed more tears of laughter at that table than most lifetimes hold. We find God more present in simple friendship than in all the formal relationships from pew to therapist's couch.

I could not lie to Lee. I don't mean the evil lies that get us in court but the common lies of everyday life where we kid ourselves and others, but not too convincingly.

I often ask others who come to see me, "Do you have anyone with whom you can say anything and know that you will not be met with instruction and reprimand, but with love and acceptance? Do you have this person in your life?" Lee and I discovered that when we asked that of people in our offices that ninety percent said they did not have such a person.

The first time I met Lee, I watched a cowboy and businessman blend come across a room toward me at a minister's luncheon. As he approached, he said the exact thing I heard in many old cowboy movies, "You're new in town," he observed.

Good grief! What is the next line? "This town is not big enough for the two of us" is what I thought he would say. Instead, without any prompting, he told me that his Baptist group was not the fundamentalist type, but the open, grace note kind.

"Grace note kind?," I asked. "I like Baptists," I replied. "I think everyone should own one!"

Lee smiled and said, "We need to have lunch. I think we could be good friends already." We had lunch and friendship for nine years.

Lee was an urban cowboy. He and his wife, Barbara, a woman who was present on the day God invented "grace," and his daughter, Debra, together shared their long-held love of horses.

They rented property. Barbara ran it. Debra worked it. Lee acted like he owned it. Love made that combination work. This family blessed everyone with their love of horses, including their church and the physically and mentally challenged.

They conducted horseback riding camps for kids in the summer. Lee told every Biblical story based on riding, cowboys and the west.

Lee was a good rider. He got me to buy a hat and good boots when everyone was doing that in the seventies. It was fashion. He was disappointed that he could not get me to fashion a love for riding as much as for wearing hat and boots. He tried.

I looked funny in the saddle. Body parts got too sore. After a long ride, I know Lee thought I was a wimp, but he never said it, which was almost worse than if he had.

Every six months, Lee and I would take an overnight trip and tell no one. We would drive to Reno. On the way, we would talk about sermon illustrations, how to make things work in the church, and tell jokes by the thousands.

When we got to Reno, we would attack the town with cowboy hats and boots and look as if we owned the place. Lee thought he did, just like the ranch he rented.

We worked the nickel machines and dreamed about the future when we would work quarter machines. We never won. But what we lost in change was worth what we got in the exchange about life, love, church, and what to preach next Sunday.

Once in Harrah's in Reno, I stepped on an elevator with Lee after the nickels ran out. We were broke and heading home. Four elderly ladies got on and eyed us with suspicion. The door closed.

Lee turned to me and broke the silence. "I told you we needed to stop betting at the $300,000 level, not at the half million level, which you just lost! Don't ever do that again or we will have to sell the ranch in Texas!"

Without thinking, I apologized. Silence again. The ladies were afraid he was going to hit me. The door opened. The ladies got off, having been in the presence of what they thought were millionaires. Lee's major in college was drama, and he always liked to test his abilities on elevators in Reno.

On the next floor, we went to the car after gambling away the ten dollars that each of our wives gave us for our weekly allowance.

The worst time ever in Reno was when Lee wandered down the street and played the penny machines. Depressing. He ended up counseling people at those machines whose lives matched their luck.

We never drove home winners, but we always drove home rich. It's that way when friendship is the reason you started a journey in the first place.

We let go of those we love slowly when they die, not all at once. Don't let others tell you how long or in what way to grieve. Grieve in your own, very personal way.

The hard part of the gospel is that we can't hear it, especially when we need to or want to. Lee's long suit was taking the gospel and putting it in a language that others could understand. He was a horseman, and on at least a hundred occasions he was asked to pray his now famous **Horseman's Prayer:**

> O Lord, Our God, as we gather in this staging area, help us to know the importance of this ride. We have been hard to load at times but at last we are ready and prepared. Guide us as we work towards safety for every rider and appreciation for the horses who carry the load. Groom us, Lord. Bring out the beauty and the best in each of us. We have reached out to you, great God, on this trail called life. You are our one and only trail boss. Forgive us when we try to ride out ahead of you, stirring up dust, and disobeying the laws of the trail. We really know better, O God. Give us a new chance. Many of us are saddled

with more than we can carry, and our sores need
your healing touch. We often become irritable and
lay our ears back and even threaten to kick each
other. Get our ears up and gentle us down. On this
ride when we jump at unknown sounds and new
ideas, rein us and control us lest we spook and hurt
someone. Help us to pause from the heat of day and
the heat of discussion for a cool and refreshing drink
from your everflowing stream. As we ride up this
mountain called life, help us to see and appreciate
the sunsets, the sunrises, full moons and the half
moons. Help us to enjoy every moment of our ride
through life. Should we stumble and fall, teach us
that underneath are the everlasting arms of you, our
trainer and owner. Make us sound to begin again,
and ride with endurance the race that is set before
us. And please, dear Lord, when you put us up for
the night, cool us down, feed us until we hunger no
more. And grant that as we come to the end of the
trail and our ride is complete that you, O God, will
help us sleep in peace and rest. May this valley be a
better place because we have passed this way. In the
name of the one who cares for us, our Lord.

Amen.

I'd rather see a sermon than hear one any day. I'd
rather see a prayer than hear one. Lee WAS the sermon,
for many, and his life IS our answered prayer.

One day, in Luciano's Italian Restaurant, Lee said,
*"The reason we don't feel the power of Easter is that we
worship a Jesus who was never dead!* We worship a Jesus
who was tastefully taken from the splendor of a Jerusa-

lem entry, to the magnificence of Easter." The sermon had begun.

"A Jesus that was never dead makes me want to puke," he said. "I want to tell people that the power of Jesus is not that he avoided all the pain we know, but that he felt it willingly in order to bring God closer to us. He was dead, Dick!"

Lee continued. "I can't get anyone to come to church on Maundy Thursday, the night we talk about his death, unless I feed them. Then, when Jesus tastefully appears again on Easter, the folk return for great music and hot cross buns!" I didn't interrupt.

Lee went on. "The only one that can be resurrected is the one who is dead! You gotta be dead first in order to be raised!" Lee leaned back in his chair. He was through.

We ordered dessert. And so does the church, every time the church faces the prospect of a dead Jesus. We like to come when dessert is served, and refuse the lima beans of Maundy Thursday and avoid the dry ham of Good Friday. We want dessert and will only come when dessert is served!

"Jesus was dead, Dick!" The message of Holy Week. Lee said it.

I walked to a lonely country cemetery one month after Lee's death, with Lee's wife. No marker yet. Just a mound. The place was cold. So was I.

The day they buried him, preachers came along with students, a seminary president, a rodeo clown, a disc jockey, and others who would have no reason to be in the same place had it not been for Lee.

Going to Lee's grave was just as awful as I expected. And after leaving, you have no idea how much I wanted to hear Lee's Luciano's sermon, "The only one that can be raised is the one who is dead."

I wanted to hear resurrection! But I didn't. I couldn't. I heard another word for the first time — Lee is dead.

Lent began that day for me.

CHRISTMAS PAGEANTS

Christmas pageants are like grace: the best ones are when the plans fall apart.

I remember a family in Northern California who put on a "living pageant" for ten years in front of a Baptist church. They quit after it became a near "living nightmare."

They would line up Joseph, Mary and the shepherds complete with a manger with a doll in it. A donkey was brought in by a local farmer along with a calf.

I think it was in the ninth year that they knew it would be their last. It seems that once they got the "live" group in place, including animals, they would leave to have coffee.

They left the scene for ten minutes and came back. They left for another twenty minutes. So far, so good. They came back thirty minutes later and noticed a logjam of cars stopped in front of the church.

Like a bad dream, they saw Joseph and Mary having a hay fight in the stable. When Joseph really wanted to do damage, he smashed Mary over the head with the doll that was supposed to be Jesus. Anyway, Joseph and Mary were going at it, with fake baby Jesus providing the best knockout punch.

Then, the guy in charge of the donkey let the donkey have too much rope. The donkey started eating the shrubs placed in the Dudley Nogle Memorial Garden right in front of the Memorial Lamp Post. Dudley loved bushes, and now they were gone.

The shepherds, meanwhile, had the bright idea of milking the cow that was left by a farmer. Those city boys never did figure out how to work that out on the baby bull! Theories ranged from pumping the tail to kicking it. No milk! And finally, the angel took her halo off and bent it into the shape of a slingshot and started peppering the neighbors roof with small rocks.

"OOOOOOOO Holy Niiiiiiiiiiiiiiiiight," went the cassette tape in the background. That was the last year of the live Christmas pageant.

But, my favorite scene still remains after eight years, when during the Christmas pageant, a little girl down in the front row of angels had trouble keeping her wire halo up. It kept slipping. Every protest of her hand bent it a little more, and it fit worse with each verse. Finally, with one giant push upward, the bent and broken sign of purity, holiness and heaven, this bent halo, came ringing around her neck as if she were a dead ringer at the county fair. Because our halos are so irretrievably bent, God bent as low as a stable, not to prod us to perfection, but to forgive the failure of our best efforts, and give us first prize anyway.

There is another pageant I will never forget. This pageant was not played out on the stage but in the mean streets of the city.

Headline at Christmas: *"Baby found in dumpster in garbage bag by man looking for cans. Baby would have died*

within minutes if not rescued. Film at eleven."
Why is it that when something like this comes on television, I no longer gasp? Have we heard this stuff so long that we cannot hear it as we should?

Here is something that did not make the headlines. In our congregation, two persons had hoped for ... prayed for a child. Continued prayers were needed for a difficult pregnancy. We prayed. We worried. Ryan was born a little early, with doctor's help and parents' permission. Ryan was sent to baby intensive care.

We danced when we heard that Ryan Jacob Heatherly, born a little early, was healthy and that his early arrival would not prevent him from getting home by Christmas! Joy to the world!

In baby intensive care, I shall never forget the double nativity. Here was a long-expected child, desired much by parents — the long-awaited gift — arriving with dancing all around. And next to Ryan, doing fine under careful observation, was Jane Doe — right there on the name plate — renamed by the hospital that greeted her as "Noel." Her name is Christmas.

There I stood between the warm greeting of parents and all that life was meant to be on one side. On the other side I saw a life rescued from a garbage dump — a life where persons other than parents would have to give to little Noel all that life was meant to be.

God bless you, Ryan. You have no idea how much we have anticipated your arrival. You have no idea what great parents are choosing to give you the very best.

God bless you, Noel. You have no idea how great life will be on the day that you become the chosen one by two people who have wanted you but could not have you on their own.

The Space Between the Notes

Babies, you came to the hospital by two different routes, but I'm here to tell you, you will both leave the same. You will both leave chosen ... chosen by love. And everyone who is chosen is at home in this world no matter how they got here and no matter where they go. Grace note!

That is the best Christmas pageant I will ever see.

EASTER

I remember clearly an early Monday morning fifteen years ago — the day after Easter. I was still in a daze over the dereliction and celebration the day before. Why can't life always be like that great day?

I had to fight the freeway traffic for two hours to get to San Francisco International Airport to pick up Jon. He had been away for a week visiting relatives. Jon is mentally retarded. In comparison to other Down's syndrome persons, his condition is not too severe.

Out of the gate, and late as usual, came Jon. He was escorted by a beautiful flight attendant who looked at least like a runner-up in a Miss Arizona contest. Jon handed me the papers that parents and relatives sign when sending a child alone on the plane.

I noted the caption on the top — a word to anyone who might seek to assist Jon: **"Note — this child is retarded."** I laughed and thought of life's little reversals. Even Jon can spell **retarded**!

Later, while waiting for luggage, I turned around to find Jon lying on the inclined baggage carousel — taking a ride. By the way he was settled between the luggage, I assumed that I saw him while he was on his third trip around. He received parental instruction, and he promised never ever in all his life to do it again. And we both knew that youthful oaths were meant to be broken.

We finally got the baggage. The sky cap assisted Jon and gave him the gifts of a smile and a warm greeting complete with southern accent. Jon told his new friend where he had been.

The sky cap vanished into the crowd. While walking toward the door, Jon informs me that he must find his friend he just met. Jon hustled through the crowd and found the sky cap and handed him the best Easter egg in his basket that I was asked to hold.

The sky cap was grateful, and Jon was aglow with the spirit. I see Easter all over again by this simple, holy exchange between Jon and the sky cap.

On the freeway heading home, while I was thinking of writing about the tender exchange I had just witnessed, Jon began to empty his pockets on the seat. He was proud that he had crammed into his pocket twenty little bars of soap that he found in the small restroom on the plane. Angel status canceled!

In the compelling novel by Morris West, the little children in the Institute in Paris have been affectionately called, les petites bouffonnes du bon Dieu ... "God's little clowns." That is Jon. That is all of us, I think — saint and shadow blended beneath an Easter smile. The Clowns of God!

And so, after all this, I neither write about Jon nor what his life says to us about Easter. Instead, I write the airlines.

"Dear Southwest Airlines. You don't know me, but as a minister I feel compelled to write you in all candor and honesty. I am aware that you have been having a

problem with people stealing your little soap bars on
your planes. Let me explain. You see my son, Jon … "

CONCLUSION

I remember the time I called on a lady who was
dying. Her husband had died two years previously, and
she was ready to die. I had spent many hours with her in
her pain and in her memory of her late husband.

When I came to see her, it was at a difficult time in
my own life, more difficult than what I would admit. I
came to her bedside, one of several calls in the day. I
greeted her and held her hand and we talked.

Then, out of nowhere, with very penetrating eyes,
she pulled me close and said, "Waiting is hard for you,
isn't it?"

Without warning I was crying uncontrollably at her
bedside while she had the good grace to say nothing.
Her word was like sacred scripture finally heard.

"You're trying too hard. What you want cannot be
created, only received. God can't work with hands that
are full," she said.

She told me about the poet Milton. She told me of
his blindness and the fact that he could not see until he
finally went blind. He saw things that could only be seen
after the distractions of trying, fixing and forcing had
died. As the dark surrounded him, he said, "And post
o'er land and ocean without rest: **They also serve who
only stand and wait.**"

In that singular moment wedged between my
striving for greatness and my despair, she gave me new
music: "They also serve who only stand and wait."

Grace Notes

The space between the notes makes the music, not the notes themselves. We only know, in looking back, that the greatest of gifts were there all along, but we did not see them at the time. The past mistake does not matter now. The power of those gifts can be received in our remembering those moments, not in nostalgia, but gratitude and grace.